P.S. God Loves You Too!

by
Connie Witter

Honor Books
Tulsa, Oklahoma

P.S. God Loves You Too!
ISBN 1-56292-452-4
Copyright © 1998 by Connie Witter
P.O. Box 3064
Broken Arrow, Oklahoma 74013-3064

Published by Honor Books
P.O. Box 55388
Tulsa, Oklahoma 74155

Cover illustration by Rachael McCampbell.

References

Contents

Introduction

Are you feeling like you just aren't getting through to God in your prayer times or do you just long for a greater understanding of His character? This book is filled with paraphrases of Scripture designed to show you that God is present and interested in all areas of your life. The Bible is His letter to you, explaining His unconditional love and forgiveness, and His desire for a beautiful relationship with you.

P.S. God Loves You Too! will make clear to you God's love and acceptance and also His never-ending faithfulness to your needs. It will reveal all the things God does to help you deal with life's tough issues and remind you that He shares the good times too. With topics on everything from marriage and success to healing and prayer, this book will surely speak to your needs. Soak in the words of Scripture and meditate on each one. Let His words fill your slow moments, your joyful moments, and your not-so-great moments. Hear God as He tells you again and again, "I love you."

*D*o you realize that I want only the best for you?
I am your Heavenly Father, and it pleases Me greatly
to see you prosper in every area of your life.

Let the LORD be magnified, which hath pleasure in the prosperity of his servant.
—PSALM 35:27 KJV

9

*I*f you will follow Me and listen to My voice, your life will overflow with My blessings, and your days will be filled with joy.

If they obey and serve him, they shall spend their days in prosperity,
and their years in pleasures.

—JOB 36:11 KJV

*C*hoose to obey My Word, and I will prosper you abundantly. Yes, I will take great delight in blessing all you do.

If you fully obey the LORD your God . . . The LORD will grant you abundant prosperity . . . and . . . bless all the work of your hands.

—DEUTERONOMY 28:1, 11–12

The Lord will again delight in prospering you.

—DEUTERONOMY 30:9 AMP

If you will give Me first place in your life and trust Me completely, I will surround you with favor. I will guide you toward My plan for your life, and you will be a great success!

If you want favor with both God and man . . . then trust the Lord completely;
don't ever trust yourself. In everything you do, put God first,
and he will direct you and crown your efforts with success.

—PROVERBS 3:4–6 TLB

I will reward you as you diligently seek Me. Be a student of My Word and search for My Wisdom; for as long as you seek Me with all your heart, I will cause you to prosper.

He is a rewarder of them that diligently seek him.

—HEBREWS 11:6 KJV

He set himself to seek God in the days of Zechariah, who instructed him in the things of God; and as long as he sought (inquired of, yearned for) the Lord, God made him prosper.

—2 CHRONICLES 26:5 AMP

*Beloved, I wish above all things that thou mayest prosper
and be in health, even as thy soul prospereth.*

—3 JOHN 2 KJV

*Despise God's Word and find yourself in trouble.
Obey it and succeed.*

—PROVERBS 13:13 TLB

14

"Only be strong and very courageous; be careful to do according to all the law; . . . do not turn from it to the right or to the left, so that you may have success wherever you go."

—JOSHUA 1:7 NAS

You are very special to Me. The angels of heaven
rejoiced the day you became My child.

*I tell you that in the same way there will be more rejoicing in heaven over one sinner
who repents than over ninety-nine righteous persons who do not need to repent.*

—LUKE 15:7

*Y*ou are My child, and I take great delight in you. Do not recall your past mistakes, for in My love, I have forgiven you and they are forgotten. Through your faith in Jesus, you stand pure and holy in My sight. I rejoice over you with singing!

The Lord your God is in the midst of you, a Mighty One, a Savior [Who saves]! He will rejoice over you with joy; He will rest [in silent satisfaction] and in His love He will be silent and make no mention [of past sins, or even recall them]; He will exult over you with singing.

—ZEPHANIAH 3:17 AMP

17

I want you to be confident and secure in the love I have for you.
As you abide in My love, I will abide in you.
You love Me, because I first loved you.

And we have known and believed the love that God hath to us. God is love;
and he that dwelleth in love dwelleth in God, and God in him.
We love him, because he first loved us.

—1 JOHN 4:16,19 KJV

18

*D*o not ever doubt My love for you. I proved how very much I loved you when I sent My Son to take the punishment for your sins. It is not because of your love for Me that I did this, but because of My great love for you.

God showed how much he loved us by sending his only Son into this wicked world to bring to us eternal life through his death. In this act we see what real love is: it is not our love for God, but his love for us when he sent his Son to satisfy God's anger against our sins.

—1 JOHN 4:9–10 TLB

19

20

"I have loved you even as the Father has loved me.
Live within my love. When you obey me you are living in my love,
just as I obey my Father and live in his love.
I have told you this so that you will be filled with my joy.
Yes, your cup of joy will overflow!"

—JOHN 15:9–11 TLB

*Long ago, even before he made the world, God chose us
to be his very own, through what Christ would do for us;
he decided then to make us holy in his eyes, without a single fault—
we who stand before him covered with his love.
So overflowing is his kindness towards us that
he took away all our sins through the blood of his Son,
by whom we are saved; and he has showered down upon us
the richness of his grace.*

—EPHESIANS 1:4,7–8 TLB

21

*D*o you realize how I long to fulfill your hopes and dreams?
Look to Me with a confident expectation, and I will open up
My hand and satisfy the desires of your heart.

Yet the LORD longs to be gracious to you . . . Blessed are all who wait for him!

—ISAIAH 30:18

You open your hand and satisfy the desires of every living thing.

—PSALM 145:16

*I*f you will only trust Me, I will grant you your heart's desire.
You are My anointed, and I will answer you when you call. I will
bring you victory through the power of My right hand.

The desire of the righteous shall be granted.

—PROVERBS 10:24 KJV

May He grant you according to your heart's desire and fulfill all your plans.
Now I know that the Lord saves His anointed; He will answer him from
His holy heaven with the saving strength of His right hand.

—PSALM 20:4,6 AMP

I know the desires of your heart. I know what you want for your family and for yourself. Have I not promised to bring them all to pass? Put your trust in Me and watch in expectation, and I will fulfill every desire of your heart.

O Lord, you have examined my heart and know everything about me.

—PSALM 139:1 TLB

He fulfills the desires of those who reverence and trust him.

—PSALM 145:19 TLB

*A*s you trust and rely upon Me, My power will be at work in you. Then I am able to bring to pass far over and above what you would ever ask for or even imagine. Yes, I will accomplish infinitely beyond your highest prayers, desires, hopes, and dreams in every area of your life.

25

Now glory be to God who by his mighty power at work within us is able to do far more than we would ever dare ask or even dream of—infinitely beyond our highest prayers, desires, thoughts, or hopes.

—EPHESIANS 3:20 TLB

Therefore I say unto you, What things soever ye desire,
when ye pray, believe that ye receive them,
and ye shall have them.

—MARK 11:24 KJV

*Delight yourself also in the Lord, and He will give you
the desires and secret petitions of your heart.
Commit your way to the Lord
[roll and repose each care of your load on Him];
trust (lean on, rely on, and be confident) also in Him
and He will bring it to pass.*

—PSALM 37:4–5 AMP

*M*y child, you can know this for sure: if you ask for anything
in agreement with My will, I hear you. And you can rest
assured that what you have asked for will come to pass,
for I am faithful to do what I have promised.

*This is the confidence we have in approaching God: that if we ask anything
according to his will, he hears us. And if we know that he hears us—
whatever we ask—we know that we have what we asked of him.*

—1 JOHN 5:14–15

*D*o not be vague or confused concerning My will, but renew your mind to My Word so that you can understand and fully grasp what My will is for you. For when you know My will, you will pray with confidence, and your prayers will be powerful and effective.

*Therefore do not be vague and thoughtless and foolish,
but understanding and firmly grasping what the will of the Lord is.*

—EPHESIANS 5:17 AMP

*Be transformed by the renewing of your mind. Then you will be able to
test and approve what God's will is—his good, pleasing and perfect will.*

—ROMANS 12:2

"What do you want me to do for you?"

—MATTHEW 20:32

Ask and you will receive, and your joy will be complete.

—JOHN 16:24

*Whatever you ask for in prayer, having faith
and [really] believing, you will receive.*

—MATTHEW 21:22 AMP

*But when he asks, he must believe and not doubt,
because he who doubts is like a wave of the sea,
blown and tossed by the wind. That man should not think he will
receive anything from the Lord.*

—JAMES 1:6–7

*C*ome into the secret place and take time to fellowship and share
your heart with Me. Set aside a special time in secret to hear
My voice, and I will bless your life for all to see.

"When you pray, go into your room, and when you have shut your door,
pray to your Father who is in the secret place; and your Father
who sees in secret will reward you openly."

—MATTHEW 6:6 NKJV

*D*on't become discouraged concerning what you have been praying for; for when you pray, My power is at work to bring to pass your heart's desire. As long as you don't give up but continue to pray, the answer will come in My perfect timing and in My perfect way.

33

[Jesus] told them a parable to the effect that they ought always to pray and not to turn coward (faint, lose heart, and give up).

LUKE 18:1 AMP

The earnest (heartfelt, continued) prayer of a righteous man makes tremendous power available [dynamic in its working].

—JAMES 5:16 AMP

34

If you live in Me [abide vitally united to Me]
and My words remain in you
and continue to live in your hearts,
ask whatever you will, and it shall be done for you.

—JOHN 15:7 AMP

"In solemn truth I tell you . . .
I am going to be with the Father.
You can ask him for anything, using my name,
and I will do it, for this will bring praise to the Father
because of what I, the Son, will do for you.
Yes, ask anything, using my name, and I will do it!"

—JOHN 14:12–14 TLB

*M*y child, lie down and sleep in peace.
You have no reason to be afraid. Rest in My
love and I will make sure you dwell in safety.

*In peace I will both lie down and sleep, for You, Lord,
alone make me dwell in safety and confident trust.*

PSALM 4:8 AMP

*M*y name is a strong tower. When you are afraid,
call upon My name and put your trust in Me.
I will protect you and keep you safe from harm.

*When I am afraid, I will trust in you. In God, whose word I praise,
in God I trust; I will not be afraid. What can mortal man do to me?*

—PSALM 56:3–4

The name of the LORD is a strong tower; the righteous run to it and are safe.

—PROVERBS 18:10

38

*D*well in My secret place by continuing to
worship and fellowship with Me, and then you shall abide
under the shadow of My wings. I will deliver you from
hidden danger and from deadly diseases. I will cover you with
My feathers, and My faithfulness will be your shield.
Therefore, you will not fear the terror of the night, nor the evil
that happens at noonday, nor the diseases that stalk in darkness,
nor the disaster that destroys at midday.

A thousand may fall at your side, ten thousand at your right hand, but it will not come near you. You will only observe with your eyes and see the punishment of the wicked. If you will dwell in My presence and make Me your place of safety and protection, then no harm will befall you, no disaster will come near your home. For I will command My angels to take charge over you and protect you in all your ways.

—PSALM 91:1–11 (AUTHOR'S PARAPHRASE)

*T*rust in Me and you will be as secure as a mountain.
No matter what comes against you, you will not be moved.
For as the mountains surround and protect Jerusalem,
so I, the Lord, will surround and protect you.

40

*Those who trust in the Lord are steady as Mount Zion, unmoved
by any circumstance. Just as the mountains surround and protect
Jerusalem, so the Lord surrounds and protects his people.*

—PSALM 125:1–2 TLB

*A*s you look to Me with confident trust, I will care for you and be your defender. I will watch over and protect you wherever you go and keep you safe from harm.

Jehovah himself is caring for you! He is your defender. He protects you day and night. He keeps you from all evil, and preserves your life. He keeps his eye upon you as you come and go, and always guards you.

—PSALM 121:5–8 TLB

42

My son, preserve sound judgment and discernment,
do not let them out of your sight . . . Then you will go
on your way in safety, and your foot will not stumble;
when you lie down, you will not be afraid;
when you lie down, your sleep will be sweet.
Have no fear of sudden disaster or of the ruin that overtakes
the wicked, for the LORD will be your confidence and
will keep your foot from being snared.

—PROVERBS 3:21,23-26

Whoever listens to me will live in safety
and be at ease, without fear of harm.

—PROVERBS 1:33

I want you to realize the grace that was given to you through My Son Jesus—He had everything, yet He gave it all up for you. Yes, He took upon Himself the curse of poverty so that you might receive the blessing of abundance.

For you are becoming progressively acquainted with and recognizing more strongly and clearly the grace of our Lord Jesus Christ . . . [in] that though He was [so very] rich, yet for your sakes He became [so very] poor, in order that by His poverty you might become enriched (abundantly supplied).

—2 CORINTHIANS 8:9 AMP

*D*o not worry about having enough money to provide for yourself. You are My child and I am aware of everything you need. If you will only trust Me and first seek My kingdom, then all the things you need will be given to you.

And do not set your heart on what you will eat or drink; do not worry about it. For the pagan world runs after all such things, and your Father knows that you need them. But seek his kingdom, and these things will be given to you as well.

—LUKE 12:29-31

I see your situation, and I know exactly what you need.
So put your trust in Me and I will show you what to do so
that your needs will be provided. Yes, I will provide
for you, just as a shepherd provides for his sheep.

The LORD is my shepherd, I shall not be in want.

—PSALM 23:1

And my God will meet all your needs according to his glorious riches in Christ Jesus.

—PHILIPPIANS 4:19

*M*y child, make this your goal in life: to live in peace and to be the best in the work you are doing. Then you will be respected by others because I will bless the work of your hands, and you will have plenty to meet all of your needs.

This should be your ambition: to live a quiet life, minding your own business and doing your own work, just as we told you before. As a result, people who are not Christians will trust and respect you, and you will not need to depend on others for enough money to pay your bills.

—1 THESSALONIANS 4:11–12 TLB

47

48

Choose my instruction instead of silver,
knowledge rather than choice gold,
for wisdom is more precious than rubies,
and nothing you desire can compare with her.
I love those who love me, and those who seek me find me.
With me are riches and honor, enduring wealth and prosperity.

—PROVERBS 8:10–11,17–18

Then I realized that it is good and proper
for a man to eat and drink,
and to find satisfaction in his toilsome labor
under the sun during the few days of life
God has given him—for this is his lot.
Moreover, when God gives any man wealth and possessions,
and enables him to enjoy them, to accept his lot and
be happy in his work—this is a gift of God.

—ECCLESIASTES 5:18–19

*B*e a faithful and wise steward over the finances that I have
blessed you with; for if you are faithful with little,
I will make you ruler over much.

You have been faithful and trustworthy over a little; I will put you in charge of much.
—MATTHEW 25:23 AMP

Moreover it is required in stewards, that a man be found faithful.
—1 CORINTHIANS 4:2 KJV

*H*onor and worship Me with the first part of your income
and I will delight in blessing you abundantly. Yes, I will
fill your storage places with plenty.

*Honor the Lord with your capital and sufficiency [from righteous labors] and with the
firstfruits of all your income; so shall your storage places be filled with plenty.*

—PROVERBS 3:9–10 AMP

*B*e a generous giver, and I will bless you abundantly.
Yes, I will pour My grace into your life so that you will have
everything you need in abundance. You will be made rich in
every way so that you can be a blessing to others.

*Whoever sows generously will also reap generously. And God is able to
make all grace abound to you, so that in all things at all times, having all
that you need, you will abound in every good work. You will be made
rich in every way so that you can be generous on every occasion.*

—2 CORINTHIANS 9:6,8,11

*M*y will for you is that you would be the lender and not the borrower. As you follow Me and trust in My promises, I will promote you to the top. You will be at the top and not at the bottom. Ask Me for wisdom, and I will give you inspired ideas and super–abundantly prosper the work of your hands.

53

If you fully obey the LORD . . . The LORD will grant you abundant prosperity . . . You will lend to many nations but will borrow from none. The LORD will make you the head, not the tail . . . you will always be at the top, never at the bottom.

—DEUTERONOMY 28:1,11–13

If any of you lacks wisdom, he should ask God . . . and it will be given to him.

—JAMES 1:5

54

"Obey the laws of the Lord your God. Walk in his ways and
fear him. For the Lord your God is bringing you into . . .
a land where food is plentiful, and nothing is lacking; . . .
But that is the time to be careful! Beware that in
your plenty you don't forget the Lord
your God and begin to disobey him.

For when you have become full and prosperous and have built fine homes to live in, and when your flocks and herds have become very large, and your silver and gold have multiplied, that is the time to watch out that you don't become proud. . . . Always remember that it is the Lord your God who gives you power to become rich, and he does it to fulfill his promise to your ancestors."

—DEUTERONOMY 8:6–7, 9, 11–14, 18 TLB

𝒜s a parent, you want all of your children to be healthy.
Why would you ever think that I would want any less for you?
You are My child, and it is My will and desire that
you would walk in health.

*Beloved, I wish above all things that thou mayest prosper
and be in health, even as thy soul prospereth.*

—3 JOHN 2 KJV

I want you to realize that Jesus took away your weaknesses. He washed away your sins. He took upon Himself your sin and your sicknesses so that you might be forgiven and be healed.

When evening came, they brought to Him many who were under the power of demons, and He drove out the spirits with a word and restored to health all who were sick. And thus He fulfilled what was spoken by the prophet Isaiah, He Himself took [in order to carry away] our weaknesses and infirmities and bore away our diseases.

—MATTHEW 8:16–17 AMP

*M*y child, if you will live in peace, this will bring health and healing to your body. But, if you allow jealousy, anger, and strife in your life, it will produce sickness. So fill your mind with My Word and begin to praise and worship Me. Then you will walk in health.

A calm and undisturbed mind and heart are the life and health of the body, but envy, jealousy, and wrath are like rottenness of the bones.

—PROVERBS 14:30 AMP

Fix your thoughts on what is true and good and right. . . . Think about all you can praise God for . . . and the God of peace will be with you.

—PHILIPPIANS 4:8-9 TLB

*R*ejoice in Me! Fill your heart with joy by praising and thanking Me for all that I have promised you. Rejoice in My love and faithfulness. For a joyful heart produces health, but a sad heart will produce sickness.

Rejoice in the Lord always [delight, gladden yourselves in Him]; again I say, Rejoice!

—PHILIPPIANS 4:4 AMP

A happy heart is good medicine and a cheerful mind works healing, but a broken spirit dries up the bones.

—PROVERBS 17:22 AMP

*"Worship the LORD your God, and his blessing
will be on your food and water. I will take away
sickness from among you, and none will miscarry or
be barren in your land. I will give you a full life span."*

—EXODUS 23:25–26

If you pay attention to these laws and are careful to follow them . . .
The LORD will keep you free from every disease.

—DEUTERONOMY 7:12,15

$\mathcal{M}$y child, reverence and worship Me as your healer, and My healing virtue will flow through you; for I am the Lord Who heals you of every sickness and every disease.

I am the Lord Who heals you.
—EXODUS 15:26 AMP

Reverently fear and worship the Lord and turn [entirely] away from evil. It shall be health to your nerves and sinews, and marrow and moistening to your bones.
—PROVERBS 3:7–8 AMP

I sent My Son to forgive all your sins and to heal all your diseases. As He walked upon this earth, many trusted in Him to heal them. And whatever their pain or illness, He healed them.

Jesus traveled all through Galilee . . . And he healed every kind of sickness and disease. . . . Sick folk were soon coming to be healed. . . . And whatever their illness or pain . . . he healed them all.

—MATTHEW 4:23–24 TLB

There is no respect of persons with God.

—ROMANS 2:11 KJV

I sent My Word to heal you and to deliver you from destruction. Put your confidence in My Word, for it will not return to Me without blessing you. It will produce healing in your body and victory in your life, for that is why I sent My Word to you.

He sends forth His word and heals them and
rescues them from the pit and destruction.

—PSALM 107:20 AMP

"So is my word that goes out from my mouth: It will not return to me empty,
but will accomplish what I desire and achieve the purpose for which I sent it."

—ISAIAH 55:11

*M*y Word contains healing power. Fill your mind with
My wisdom, My promises and My love and faithfulness.
Keep My Word deep within your heart, and it will bring you life.
Yes, it will bring health and healing to your whole body.

My son, attend to my words; consent and submit to my sayings.
Let them not depart from your sight; keep them in the center of your heart.
For they are life to those who find them, healing and health to all their flesh.

—PROVERBS 4:20–22 AMP

66

*Is any one of you sick? He should call for the elders
of the church to pray over him and anoint him with oil
in the name of the Lord. And the prayer offered in faith
will make the sick person well; the Lord will raise him up.*

—JAMES 5:14–15

Go ye into all the world, and preach the gospel to every creature.
He that believeth and is baptized shall be saved . . .
And these signs shall follow them that believe;
In my name shall they cast out devils;
they shall speak with new tongues; . . .
they shall lay hands on the sick,
and they shall recover.

—MARK 16:15–18 KJV

*M*y child, put your complete trust in Me. Do not continue to worry and fret over decisions you need to make. Quit relying upon yourself and your own wisdom. If you will only rely on Me and ask Me to guide you, I will lead you down the right path.

Do not be anxious about anything, but in everything, by prayer and petition, with thanksgiving, present your requests to God.

—PHILIPPIANS 4:6

Trust in the LORD with all thine heart; and lean not unto thine own understanding. In all thy ways acknowledge him, and he shall direct thy paths.

—PROVERBS 3:5–6 KJV

I will guide you along the path I have for your life. I will open your understanding so that you might know which way to go. What seems hard and confusing, I will make smooth and easy. Yes, as you trust Me, I will do this for you. I will not fail you.

"I will lead the blind by ways they have not known, along unfamiliar paths I will guide them; I will turn the darkness into light before them and make the rough places smooth. These are the things I will do; I will not forsake them."

—ISAIAH 42:16

I am your Shepherd, and I call you by name. I walk before you and guide you in the way you should go. You will not follow the voice of the enemy. When you hear My voice leading you, you will follow it because you know My voice.

70

"He calls his own sheep by name and leads them out. When he has brought out all his own, he goes on ahead of them, and his sheep follow him because they know his voice. But they will never follow a stranger; in fact, they will run away from him because they do not recognize a stranger's voice."

—JOHN 10:3-5

I will guide you always. I will give you wisdom and fulfill
your every need. I will strengthen you, and your life
will produce abundant fruit. Yes, if you will only
put your trust in Me, I will not let you fail.

*"The LORD will guide you always; he will satisfy your needs in a
sun-scorched land and will strengthen your frame. You will be like a
well-watered garden, like a spring whose waters never fail."*

—ISAIAH 58:11

*I will instruct you (says the Lord) and guide you
along the best pathway for your life;
I will advise you and watch your progress.*

—PSALM 32:8 TLB

*"I am the LORD your God, who teaches you what is best
for you, who directs you in the way you should go."*

—ISAIAH 48:17

*Roll your works upon the Lord [commit
and trust them wholly to Him;
He will cause your thoughts
to become agreeable to His will,
and] so shall your plans be established and succeed.*

—PROVERBS 16:3 AMP

*D*o not worry about your family's salvation. Put your trust in Me, and all of your family will be saved. You can rest assured that I will draw them to Myself and give them the desire to come to Jesus; for I am well able to do what I have promised.

"Believe in the Lord Jesus, and you will be saved—you and your household."

—ACTS 16:31

No one is able to come to Me unless the Father Who sent Me attracts and draws him and gives him the desire to come to Me.

—JOHN 6:44 AMP

*P*ray and intercede for your family's salvation; for My Word
says that I will deliver those for whom you pray. Yes,
I will deliver them from the powers of darkness and
will bring them into the kingdom of My Son.

*He will even deliver the one [for whom you intercede] who is not innocent;
yes, he will be delivered through the cleanness of your hands.*

—JOB 22:30 AMP

*Giving thanks unto the Father . . . Who hath delivered us from the power of darkness,
and hath translated us into the kingdom of his dear Son.*

—COLOSSIANS 1:12–13 KJV

75

76

*I*t pleases Me when you pray for the salvation of your family; for it is My will that they would be saved and come to the knowledge of the truth.

I urge, then, first of all, that requests, prayers, intercession and thanksgiving be made for everyone. . . . This is good, and pleases God our Savior, who wants all men to be saved and to come to a knowledge of the truth.

—1 TIMOTHY 2:1,3-4

*A*sk Me to send laborers across their paths. As others begin to tell them about Jesus, I will open up the eyes of their understanding and reveal My love for them; for it is My lovingkindness that will draw them to repentance.

"Ask the Lord of the harvest, therefore, to send out workers into his harvest field."
—MATTHEW 9:38

God's kindness leads you toward repentance.
—ROMANS 2:4

*T*he salvation of your family may seem impossible to you. But remember, what seems impossible to man is possible with Me; for all things are possible if you will only believe.

"Who then can be saved?" Jesus looked at them and said, "With man this is impossible, but with God all things are possible."

—MATTHEW 19:25–26

Jesus said unto him, If thou canst believe, all things are possible to him that believeth.

—MARK 9:23 KJV

*P*ut your confidence in the power of My influence,
and My grace will be effectively at work in your family's life.
Yes, I will exert My holy influence upon their minds, wills,
and emotions and turn them toward Christ and draw
them to Myself with lovingkindness.

*The grace of God (the unmerited favor and merciful kindness by which God,
exerting His holy influence upon souls, turns them to Christ, and
keeps, strengthens, and increases them in Christian virtues).*

—2 CORINTHIANS 1:12 AMP

Foolishness is bound up in the heart of a child,
but the rod of discipline will drive it far from him.

—PROVERBS 22:15 AMP

The rod and reproof give wisdom, but a child left undisciplined brings his mother to shame. Correct your son, and he will give you rest; yes, he will give delight to your heart.

—PROVERBS 29:15,17 AMP

82

*P*ut My commandments within your heart. Then teach and impress them diligently upon the minds and hearts of your children. Surround them with My Word! Talk about it when you sit in your house, and when you're driving in your car, and before they go to bed, and when they wake up. Train your children to follow My ways, and when they have grown they will not depart from it.

These commandments that I give you today are to be upon your hearts. Impress them on your children. Talk about them when you sit at home and when you walk along the road, when you lie down and when you get up.

—DEUTERONOMY 6:6-7

Train up a child in the way he should go: and when he is old, he will not depart from it.

—PROVERBS 22:6 KJV

*T*ake great delight in My commandments.
Walk in My ways. Then I will pour My blessings
upon your children, and they shall be strong and blessed.

83

Praise the LORD. Blessed is the man who fears the LORD, who finds
great delight in his commands. His children will be mighty
in the land; the generation of the upright will be blessed.

—PSALM 112:1-2

*"I am the LORD; those who hope in me will not be disappointed. . . .
I will contend with those who contend with you,
and your children I will save."*

—ISAIAH 49:23,25

The seed of the righteous shall be delivered.

—PROVERBS 11:21 KJV

84

Thus says the Lord: Restrain your voice
from weeping and your eyes from tears,
for your work shall be rewarded, says the Lord;
and [your children] shall return from the enemy's land.
And there is hope for your future, says the Lord;
your children shall come back to their own country.

—JEREMIAH 31:16–17 AMP

*B*elieve what I have promised you, and I will pour
My Spirit upon your children and bless them abundantly!
They will prosper like trees planted near streams of living
water, and they will rise up and say, "I belong to the Lord!"

*I will pour out my Spirit on your offspring, and my blessing on your descendants. They
will spring up like grass in a meadow, like poplar trees by flowing streams. One will
say, "I belong to the LORD" . . . still another will write on his hand, "The Lord's."*

—ISAIAH 44:3–5

*T*his is My promise to you concerning your children—
My Spirit who is on you will also be on your children, and they
will turn from evil and want to do good. And My Word that comes
from your mouth will also be spoken by your children and your
grandchildren from this time on and forever!

"As for me, this is my covenant with them," says the LORD. *"My Spirit,
who is on you, and my words that I have put in your mouth will not depart
from your mouth, or from the mouths of your children, or from the mouths
of their descendants from this time on and forever," says the* LORD.

—ISAIAH 59:21

I know you face challenges in raising your children. But if you'll ask Me for wisdom, I will show you how to effectively handle the situations you face. Don't grow weary in training and disciplining them, for in due season you will reap a harvest of blessing in their lives.

If any of you lacks wisdom, he should ask God, who gives generously to all without finding fault, and it will be given to him.

—JAMES 1:5

Let us not get tired of doing what is right, for after a while we will reap a harvest of blessing if we don't get discouraged and give up.

—GALATIANS 6:9 TLB

*A*s you pray for your children, I will be at work in their lives. Yes, I will create in them the desire and ability to choose and to do what pleases Me.

It is God Who is all the while effectually at work in you [energizing and creating in you the power and desire], both to will and to work for His good pleasure and satisfaction and delight.

—PHILIPPIANS 2:13 AMP

90

Jesus said . . . I give you a new commandment:
that you should love one another. Just as I
have loved you, so you too should love one
another. By this shall all [men] know that you
are My disciples, if you love one another.

—JOHN 13:31,34–35 AMP

*But Jesus said . . . For this reason a man shall leave [behind]
his father and his mother and be joined to his wife
and cleave closely to her permanently,
and the two shall become one flesh,
so that they are no longer two, but one flesh.
What therefore God has united (joined together),
let not man separate or divide.*

—MARK 10:5,7-9 AMP

I made My will for your marriage very clear in My Word.
Husbands are to love their wives as Christ loves the church.
They are to cherish them, care for them, and protect them. Wives
are to reverence their husbands by honoring, praising, and loving
them. My will does not change. This was My plan for every
husband and wife before the foundation of the world.

Husbands, love your wives, as Christ loved the church and gave Himself up for her . . .
He who loves his own wife loves himself. For no man ever hated his own flesh, but
nourishes and carefully protects and cherishes it, as Christ does the church . . .
And let the wife see that she respects and reverences her husband.

—EPHESIANS 5:25,28–29,33 AMP

*T*his is the confidence you can have in Me: if you'll pray and ask Me to bring to pass My will in your marriage, I will do it! Yes, I will work effectually within you and your spouse and create the desire and ability to become the husband and wife that I have called you to be.

93

This is the confidence we have in approaching God: that if we ask anything according to his will, he hears us. And if we know that he hears us— whatever we ask—we know that we have what we asked of him.

—1 JOHN 5:14–15

For it is God who works in you to will and to act according to his good purpose.

—PHILIPPIANS 2:13

*If thou wilt not hearken unto the voice of the LORD thy God,
to observe to do all his commandments . . . all these curses
shall come upon thee . . . the man that is tender among you . . .
his eye shall be evil . . . toward the wife of his bosom . . .
The tender and delicate woman among you . . . her eye
shall be evil toward the husband of her bosom.*

—DEUTERONOMY 28:15,54,56 KJV

(Jesus paid the price for you to be free from this curse upon your marriage; for God's Word says): *"Christ redeemed us from the curse of the law by becoming a curse for us, for it is written: 'Cursed is everyone who is hung on a tree.' He redeemed us in order that the blessing given to Abraham might come to the Gentiles through Christ Jesus."*

—GALATIANS 3:13–14

95

*B*egin to thank Me that I am at work inside both you and your spouse even when you can't see anything happening. Your faith will grow strong as you continue to praise Me, and you will be fully persuaded that I am well able to do what I have promised.

96

But Abraham never doubted. He believed God, for his faith and trust grew ever stronger, and he praised God for this blessing even before it happened. He was completely sure that God was well able to do anything he promised.

—ROMANS 4:20–21 TLB

*M*y child, nothing is impossible with Me; for I can change the heart of a king. Because of Jesus, My miracle-working, life-changing power is available to work in your situation. Yes, I will heal, restore, and bless your marriage, if you'll only put your trust in Me.

For with God nothing is ever impossible and no word from God shall be without power or impossible of fulfillment.

—LUKE 1:37 AMP

The king's heart is in the hand of the Lord as are the watercourses; He turns it whichever way He wills.

—PROVERBS 21:1 AMP

You married women, be submissive to your own husbands . . .
so that even if any do not obey the Word [of God], they may be
won over not by discussion but by the [godly] lives of their wives,
When they observe the pure and modest way in which you conduct
yourselves, together with your reverence [for your husband;
you are to feel for him all that reverence includes: to respect,
defer to, revere him—to honor, esteem, appreciate, prize, and,
in the human sense, to adore him, that is, to admire, praise,
be devoted to, deeply love, and enjoy your husband].

—1 PETER 3:1–2 AMP

*A capable, intelligent and virtuous woman—who is he
who can find her? . . . The heart of her husband trusts
in her confidently . . . She comforts, encourages, and
does him only good as long as there is life within her.
Her husband is known in the [city's] gates, when
he sits among the elders of the land. . . . Her husband
boasts of and praises her, [saying], Many daughters
have done virtuously . . . but you excel them all. . . .
A woman who reverently and worshipfully
fears the Lord, she shall be praised!*

—PROVERBS 31:10–12, 23, 28–30 AMP

I want you to realize that as husband and wife you are joint heirs of My grace. You have tremendous authority over one another in the spirit; for you are not two, but one flesh. So speak My Word over yourself and your spouse and believe that it will come to pass, and just as I promised, you will have what you say!

In the same way you married men should live considerately with [your wives] . . . [realizing that you] are joint heirs of the grace (God's unmerited favor) of life.

—1 PETER 3:7 AMP

For verily I say unto you, That whosoever shall say . . . and shall not doubt in his heart, but shall believe that those things which he saith shall come to pass; he shall have whatsoever he saith.

—MARK 11:23 KJV

*H*umble yourself before Me and ask Me to work in you and
I will change you into the spouse that I have called you to be.
As you begin to love your spouse with My unconditional love,
I am able to bring to pass far over and above what you could
ever pray, dream, or desire in your marriage relationship.

*Now to Him Who, by (in consequence of) the [action of His] power that is
at work within us, is able to [carry out His purpose and] do superabundantly,
far over and above all that we [dare] ask or think [infinitely beyond
our highest prayers, desires, thoughts, hopes, or dreams].*

—EPHESIANS 3:20 AMP

102

Blessed are all who fear the LORD, who walk in his ways.
You will eat the fruit of your labor; blessings and
prosperity will be yours. Your wife will be like
a fruitful vine within your house; your sons
will be like olive shoots around your table.
Thus is the man blessed who fears the LORD.

—PSALM 128:1–4

"I am the LORD, the God of all mankind. Is anything too hard for me?"
—JEREMIAH 32:27

103

"All things are possible to him who believes."
—MARK 9:23 NKJV

*I*f you'll confess your sins with a sincere heart, I am faithful to forgive you and cleanse you from all unrighteousness. Not only will I forgive your sins, but I will completely and permanently forget them.

If we confess our sins, he is faithful and just and will forgive us our sins and purify us from all unrighteousness.

—1 JOHN 1:9

"I will forgive their wickedness and will remember their sins no more."

—HEBREWS 8:12

*O*nce you've asked for forgiveness, do not continue to feel guilty. But rejoice in My promise, for your sins have been erased, and I will not count them against you.

What happiness for those whose guilt has been forgiven! . . .
What relief for those who have confessed their sins
and God has cleared their record.

—PSALM 32:1–2 TLB

*A*s far as the heavens are above the earth, so great is the love that I have for you. And as far as the east is from the west, so I have taken your sins and removed them far from you.

He does not treat us as our sins deserve or repay us according to our iniquities. For as high as the heavens are above the earth, so great is his love for those who fear him; as far as the east is from the west, so far has he removed our transgressions from us.

—PSALM 103:10–12

I chose you and called you to come unto Me. When you came and accepted Jesus as your Savior, I declared you "not guilty!" I washed you clean with His blood and filled you with His goodness.

And having chosen us, he called us to come to him; and when we came,
he declared us "not guilty," filled us with Christ's goodness,
gave us right standing with himself, and promised us his glory.

—ROMANS 8:30 TLB

107

108

I made you, and I will not forget to help you.
I've blotted out your sins;
they are gone like morning mist at noon!
Oh, return to me, for I have
paid the price to set you free.

—ISAIAH 44:21–22 TLB

*"Brothers! Listen! In this man Jesus,
there is forgiveness for your sins!
Everyone who trusts in him is freed
from all guilt and declared righteous."*

—ACTS 13:38–39 TLB

*W*hen you feel weak, My grace is sufficient to strengthen you. My power shows itself most effective when it turns your weaknesses into strengths. For when you are weak in your flesh, My grace will make you strong!

But he said to me, "My grace is sufficient for you, for my power is made perfect in weakness." Therefore I will boast all the more gladly about my weaknesses, so that Christ's power may rest on me. . . . For when I am weak, then I am strong.

—2 CORINTHIANS 12:9–10

*Y*ou try to do things in your own strength and ability. Yet, all the time My Spirit yearns within you waiting for an invitation, waiting for you to ask for My help. Ask Me to strengthen you; for My grace is available if you are only humble enough to receive it.

The Spirit Whom He has called to dwell in us yearns over us and He yearns for the Spirit [to be welcome] with a jealous love. But He gives us more and more grace (power of the Holy Spirit, to meet this evil tendency and all others fully). That is why He says, God sets Himself against the proud . . . but gives grace [continually] to . . . (those who are humble enough to receive it).

—JAMES 4:5-6 AMP

*W*hen you need to be strengthened, come boldly to My throne
of grace, and I will give you mercy and forgiveness
for your failures and grace to overcome.

Let us then approach the throne of grace with confidence, so that
we may receive mercy and find grace to help us in our time of need.

—HEBREWS 4:16

*B*y My grace I will strengthen you and make you what you ought to be. I will equip you with everything you need to do My will. Yes, I will work in you and accomplish what is pleasing in My sight as you put your trust in Jesus.

Now may the God of peace . . . Strengthen (complete, perfect) and make you what you ought to be and equip you with everything good that you may carry out His will; [while He Himself] works in you and accomplishes that which is pleasing in His sight, through Jesus Christ.

—HEBREWS 13:20-21 AMP

113

I will sanctify you and change you into everything I have called you to be. You can trust Me completely! I have called you to fulfill a special purpose. You can rest assured that I will also bring it to pass. Yes, I will complete it!

And may the God of peace Himself sanctify you through and through [separate you from profane things, make you pure and wholly consecrated to God]. . . . Faithful is He Who is calling you [to Himself] and utterly trustworthy, and He will also do it [fulfill His call by hallowing and keeping you].

—1 THESSALONIANS 5:23–24 AMP

*W*hen you receive My grace and walk in righteousness,
you will reign as a king in life. You will walk in victory and
experience the abundant life that My Son Jesus came to give you.

*Much more surely will those who receive [God's] overflowing grace (unmerited favor)
and the free gift of righteousness . . . reign as kings in life through the one Man
Jesus Christ (the Messiah, the Anointed One).*

—ROMANS 5:17 AMP

115

*They will be my people, and I will be their God. . . . I will make
an everlasting covenant with them: I will never stop doing good to them,
and I will inspire them to fear me. . . . I will rejoice in doing them good
and . . . I will give them all the prosperity I have promised them.*

—JEREMIAH 32:38,40–42

*"I will never completely take away my lovingkindness from them,
nor let my promise fail. No, I will not break my covenant;
I will not take back one word of what I said."*

—PSALM 89:33–34 TLB

*For He [God] Himself has said, I will not in any way
fail you nor give you up nor leave you without support.
[I will] not, [I will] not, [I will] not in any degree
leave you helpless nor forsake nor let [you] down
(relax My hold on you)! [Assuredly not!]*

—Hebrews 13:5 AMP

117

*J*am your Heavenly Father and you can trust Me completely; for I am faithful, reliable, trustworthy, and true to My promises. You can depend on Me to do what I have said, for I will not allow My Word to prove false nor will I let it fail.

God is faithful (reliable, trustworthy, and therefore ever true to His promise, and He can be depended on).

—1 CORINTHIANS 1:9 AMP

What a God he is! How perfect in every way! All his promises prove true.

—PSALM 18:30 TLB

*M*y child, put your complete trust in Me and walk
in obedience to My Word. Then surely you shall feed
upon My faithfulness. Yes, you will partake of all
of My promises and be completely satisfied.

*Trust (lean on, rely on, and be confident) in the Lord and do good; so shall you
dwell in the land and feed surely on His faithfulness, and truly you shall be fed.*

—PSALM 37:3 AMP

Yes, I have spoken, and I will bring it to pass;
I have purposed it, and I will do it.

—ISAIAH 46:11 AMP

For I am alert and active,
watching over My Word to perform it.

—JEREMIAH 1:12 AMP

*Know, recognize, and understand therefore that
the Lord your God, He is God, the faithful God,
Who keeps covenant and steadfast love and mercy
with those who love Him and keep His commandments,
to a thousand generations.*

—DEUTERONOMY 7:9 AMP

I have bound Myself with an oath, so that you can be confident
and never need to wonder whether I might change My mind.
I would never lie to you. I have given you both My promise
and My oath—two things you can completely count on—
for it is impossible for My Word to prove false.

God also bound himself with an oath, so that those he promised to help would be
perfectly sure and never need to wonder whether he might change his plans.
He has given us both his promise and his oath, two things we can
completely count on, for it is impossible for God to tell a lie.

—HEBREWS 6:17–18 TLB

You are My child and if you will only put your trust in My Word, you will flourish like a palm tree. Yes, you will be a living testimony to prove that I am upright and faithful to My promises, for there is no unrighteousness in Me.

The [uncompromisingly] righteous shall flourish like the palm tree . . . they shall be full of sap [of spiritual vitality] and [rich in the] verdure [of trust, love, and contentment]. [They are living memorials] to show that the Lord is upright and faithful to His promises; He is my Rock, and there is no unrighteousness in Him.

—PSALM 92:12,14–15 AMP

124

Fear not [there is nothing to fear], for I am with you;
do not look around you in terror and be dismayed,
for I am your God. I will strengthen and harden
you to difficulties, yes, I will help you; yes,
I will hold you up and retain you with
My [victorious] right hand of
rightness and justice.

—ISAIAH 41:10 AMP

For no temptation (no trial regarded as enticing to sin) . . .
has overtaken you and laid hold on you that is not common to man. . . .
God is faithful [to His Word and to His compassionate nature],
and He [can be trusted] not to let you be tempted and tried
and assayed beyond your ability and strength
of resistance and power to endure, but with the temptation
He will [always] also provide the way out.

—1 CORINTHIANS 10:13 AMP

125

*W*hen you call to Me and ask Me for strength, I will answer you! Yes, I will fill you with My strength.

On the day I called Thou didst answer me;
Thou didst make me bold with strength in my soul.

—PSALM 138:3 NAS

The LORD gives strength to his people.

—PSALM 29:11

*T*hough you may be surrounded by troubles, I will bring you
safely through them. Put your trust in Me, My child,
for I know how to deliver you out of all your trials.

Though I am surrounded by troubles, you will bring me safely through them.
—PSALM 138:7 TLB

The Lord knows how to rescue godly men from trials.
—2 PETER 2:9

*These trials are only to test your faith,
to see whether or not it is strong and pure.
It is being tested as fire tests gold and purifies it
—and your faith is far more precious to God than mere gold;
so if your faith remains strong
after being tried in the test tube of fiery trials,
it will bring you much praise
and glory and honor on the day of his return.*

—1 PETER 1:7 TLB

128

*I am God, your God. Call on Me in the day of trouble;
I will deliver you, and you shall honor and glorify Me.*

—PSALM 50:7,15 AMP

129

*Y*ou can rejoice in your trials when you realize that their purpose is to test your faith. You will grow strong and steadfast and after patience has done a perfect work in you, you will come through your trial victoriously, not lacking any good thing.

Consider it pure joy, my brothers, whenever you face trials of many kinds, because you know that the testing of your faith develops perseverance. Perseverance must finish its work so that you may be mature and complete, not lacking anything.

—JAMES 1:2−4

*Y*ou will be blessed, happy, and envied when you remain steadfast as your faith is tested. For when your faith has proven genuine, you will receive the victor's crown of life. Yes, this is what I've promised you, so remain strong in faith and you will walk in victory in every area of your life.

Blessed (happy, to be envied) is the man who is patient under trial and stands up under temptation, for when he has stood the test and been approved, he will receive [the victor's] crown of life which God has promised to those who love Him.

—JAMES 1:12 AMP

132

*Your strength must come from the Lord's mighty power
within you. Put on all of God's armor
so that you will be able to stand safe
against all the strategies and tricks of Satan.
Use every piece of God's armor to resist the enemy
whenever he attacks, and when it is all over,
you will still be standing up.*

—EPHESIANS 6:10–11,13 TLB

*Praise the LORD. Blessed is the man who fears the LORD,
who finds great delight in his commands. He will have no fear
of bad news; his heart is steadfast, trusting in the LORD.
His heart is secure, he will have no fear; in the end
he will look in triumph on his foes.*

—PSALM 112:1,7-8

134

*M*y child, trials will come against you, and your faith will be
tested. But even in the midst of them you can rejoice in My
faithfulness, for I have promised to deliver you out of them all.

A righteous man may have many troubles, but the LORD delivers him from them all.

—PSALM 34:19

*A*braham, David, Daniel, King Jehoshaphat, Moses, and Paul chose to worship Me in the midst of their trials and I brought them through in victory. So offer up to Me a sacrifice of praise, My child, and I will do the same for you!

135

By him therefore let us offer the sacrifice of praise to God continually, that is, the fruit of our lips giving thanks to his name.

—HEBREWS 13:15 KJV

*Have I not commanded you? Be strong and courageous.
Do not be terrified; do not be discouraged.*

—JOSHUA 1:9

I will not fail you or forsake you.

—JOSHUA 1:5 AMP

"I am the Lord; those who hope in me will not be disappointed."

—ISAIAH 49:23

*M*y child, don't be so gloomy and discouraged. But, continue
to trust in Me. Worship and praise Me, for I will not fail you.
As you fill your heart with My Word and think upon
My promises, your heart will overflow with joy.

O my soul, why be so gloomy and discouraged? Trust in God! I shall again praise
him for his wondrous help; he will make me smile again, for he is my God!

—PSALM 43:5 TLB

"These things I have spoken to you, that My joy may
remain in you, and that your joy may be full."

—JOHN 15:11 NKJV

*A*s you worship and trust in Me, I will fill your heart
with joy and peace. Yes, you will overflow with
hope by the power of My Spirit.

May the God of hope fill you with all joy and peace as you trust in him,
so that you may overflow with hope by the power of the Holy Spirit.

—ROMANS 15:13

140

O my soul, don't be discouraged. Don't be upset.
Expect God to act! For I know that I shall again have plenty
of reason to praise him for all that he will do.
He is my help! He is my God!

—PSALM 42:11 TLB

*Arise [from the depression and prostration in which
circumstances have kept you—rise to a new life]!
Shine (be radiant with the glory of the Lord) . . .
the Lord shall arise upon you . . .
and His glory shall be seen on you.*

—ISAIAH 60:1–2 AMP

*D*on't throw away your confidence in Me. I will not fail you!
Continue to persevere in doing My will, and you will receive
what I have promised you. Yes, it will be worth the wait!

So do not throw away your confidence; it will be richly rewarded.
You need to persevere so that when you have done the will of God,
you will receive what he has promised.

—HEBREWS 10:35–36

*D*o not let go of My promises; for all who put their faith in My Word will be tested. So follow the example of those who refused to give up. Make a decision that you will stand on My Word no matter how long it takes, and you will partake of all that I have promised.

Follow the example of those who receive all that God has promised them because of their strong faith and patience.

—HEBREWS 6:12 TLB

*He gives strength to the weary and increases the power of the weak.
Those who hope in the Lord will renew their strength. They will
soar on wings like eagles; they will run and not grow weary,
they will walk and not be faint.*

—ISAIAH 40:29,31

*And let us not get tired of doing what is right, for after a while we will
reap a harvest of blessing if we don't get discouraged and give up.*

—GALATIANS 6:9 TLB

*Trusting means looking forward to getting something
we don't yet have—for a man who already has something
doesn't need to hope and trust that he will get it.
But if we must keep trusting God for something
that hasn't happened yet,
it teaches us to wait patiently and confidently.*

—ROMANS 8:24–25 TLB

*And patience develops strength of character in us and helps us
trust God more each time we use it until finally our hope
and faith are strong and steady.*

—ROMANS 5:4 TLB

145

146

Don't be impatient for the Lord to act!
Keep traveling steadily along his pathway and in due season
he will honor you with every blessing.

—PSALM 37:34 TLB

*[What would have become of me] had I not believed that
I would see the Lord's goodness in the land of the living!
Wait and hope for and expect the Lord; be brave and of
good courage and let your heart be stout and enduring.
Yes, wait for and hope for and expect the Lord.*

—PSALM 27:13–14 AMP

148

hy are you worrying instead of trusting Me? Did I not
tell you in My Word to cast all your cares and concerns on Me?
If you will only replace your thoughts of worry with thoughts
of My promises, you will have My perfect peace.

*Casting the whole of your care [all your anxieties, all your worries,
all your concerns, once and for all] on Him, for He cares
for you affectionately and cares about you watchfully.*

—1 PETER 5:7 AMP

*M*y child, do not worry about anything! Simply ask Me for whatever you need. Begin to lift your voice with thanksgiving; and My peace, which passes all understanding, will keep your heart and mind at rest as you trust in Christ Jesus.

149

Do not be anxious about anything, but in everything, by prayer and petition, with thanksgiving, present your requests to God. And the peace of God, which transcends all understanding, will guard your hearts and your minds in Christ Jesus.

—PHILIPPIANS 4:6-7

150

"I tell you the truth, my Father will give you whatever you ask
in my name. . . . Ask and you will receive,
and your joy will be complete. I have told you these things,
so that in me you may have peace.
In this world you will have trouble. But take heart!
I have overcome the world."

—JOHN 16:23,24–33

You will guard him and keep him in perfect and constant peace whose mind . . . is stayed on You, because he commits himself to You, leans on You, and hopes confidently in You.

—ISAIAH 26:3 AMP

*W*hen you hold unforgiveness in your heart toward someone,
you hinder My blessings from flowing into your life.
So forgive those who have done you wrong. Then you
will be forgiven, and your prayers will be answered.

"And whenever you stand praying, if you have anything against anyone, forgive him,
that your Father in heaven may also forgive you your trespasses. But if you do
not forgive, neither will your Father in heaven forgive your trespasses."

—MARK 11:25–26 NKJV

*I*t is My love that draws men to repentance, and My love lives in your heart. You have the ability to show My love to those who have hurt you. My love in you does not dwell on the sins of others; it pays no attention to a suffered wrong. So do not be overcome by evil but overcome evil with good.

(God's love in us) does not insist on its own rights or its own way, for it is not self–seeking; it is not touchy or fretful or resentful; it takes no account of the evil done to it [it pays no attention to a suffered wrong].

—1 CORINTHIANS 13:5 AMP

Do not be overcome by evil, but overcome evil with good.

—ROMANS 12:21

153

154

Never return evil for evil or insult for insult . . . but on the contrary
blessing [praying for their welfare, happiness, and protection,
and truly pitying and loving them]. For know that to this
you have been called, that you may yourselves inherit a blessing
[from God—that you may obtain a blessing as heirs,
bringing welfare and happiness and protection] . . .
search for peace . . . and seek it eagerly.

—1 PETER 3:9,11 AMP

*If you are angry, don't sin by nursing your grudge.
Don't let the sun go down with you still angry—
get over it quickly; for when you are angry you give a mighty foothold
to the devil. Don't use bad language.
Say only what is good and helpful to those you are talking to,
and what will give them a blessing.
Stop being mean, bad-tempered and angry.
Quarreling, harsh words, and dislike of others
should have no place in your lives.
Instead, be kind to each other, tenderhearted,
forgiving one another,
just as God has forgiven you because you belong to Christ.*

—EPHESIANS 4:26-27,29,31-32 TLB

156

"Love your enemies, do good to those who hate you,
bless those who curse you, pray for those who mistreat you.
If you love those who love you, what credit is that to you?
Even 'sinners' love those who love them.
And if you do good to those who are good to you, what credit is that
to you? Even 'sinners' do that. But love your enemies,
do good to them. . . . Then your reward will be great,
and you will be sons of the Most High, because
He is kind to the ungrateful and wicked.
Be merciful, just as your Father is merciful."

—LUKE 6:27-28,32-33,35-36

About the Author

Connie Witter has been a Christian since she was six years old. She believes that developing a strong relationship with God through studying His Word and prayer is essential to living a victorious Christian life. Connie has taught home Bible studies and is the author of a Bible study entitled, "God's Great and Precious Promises." In it, she teaches how she received victory in her own life through putting her absolute trust in the promises of God's Word.

Connie is married to a wonderful husband, Tony, and is the mother of three beautiful children, Justin, Jared, and Kristen. They make their home in Broken Arrow, Oklahoma.

Other titles by Connie Witter include:

God's Great and Precious Promises
Love Letters from God
P.S. God Loves You!

To contact the author, write:

Connie Witter
P.O. Box 3064
Broken Arrow, Oklahoma 74013-3064

*Additional copies of this book and other titles by Connie Witter
are available from your local bookstore.*

Honor Books
Tulsa, Oklahoma